Tertullian

On Prayer

Tertullian

On Prayer

Tertullian
On Prayer

Published by
Lighthouse Christian Publishing
SAN 257-4330
5531 Dufferin Drive
Savage, Minnesota, 55378
United States of America

www.lighthousechristianpublishing.com

Tertullian

Introductory Note.

The Second Class of Tertullian's works, according to the logical method I have endeavored to carry out, is that which includes his treatises against the heresies of his times. In these, the genius of our author is brilliantly illustrated, while, in melancholy fact, he is demonstrating the folly of his own final lapse and the wickedness of that schism and heresy into which he fell away from Truth. Were it not that history abounds in like examples of the frailty of the human intellect and of the insufficiency of "man that walketh to direct his steps," we should be forced to a theory of mental decay to account for inconsistencies so gross and for delusions so besotted. "Genius to madness is *indeed* allied," and who knows but something like that imbecility which closed the career of Swift may have been the fate of this splendid wit and versatile man of parts? Charity, admiration and love force this inquiry upon my own mind continually, as I explore his fascinating pages. And the order in which the student will find them in this series, will lead, I think, to similar reflections on the part of many readers. We observe a natural bent and turn of mind, even in his Catholic writings, which indicate his perils. These are more and more apparent in his recent works, as his enthusiasm heats itself into a frenzy which at last becomes a rage. He breaks down by degrees, as in orthodoxy so also in force and in character. It is almost like the collapse of Solomon or of Bacon. And though our own times have produced no example of stars of equal magnitude, to become falling-stars, we have seen illustrations the most humiliating, of those calm words of Bishop Kaye: "Human nature often presents the curious phenomenon of a union of the most opposite qualities in the same mind; of vigor, acuteness and discrimination on some subjects, with imbecility, dullness and bigotry on others." Milton, himself another example of his own threnode, breaks forth in this splendid utterance of lyrical confession:

"God of our fathers what is man?
Nor do I name of men the common rout,
That, wandering loose about,
Grow up and perish as the summer fly,
Heads without name, no more remembered,
But such as thou hast solemnly elected,
With gifts and graces eminently adorned,
To some great work, thy glory
And people's safety, *which in part they effect*."

And here, I must venture a remark on the ambiguity of the expressions concerning our author's Montanism. In the treatise against Marcion, written late in his career, Tertullian identifies himself with the Church and strenuously defends its faith and its apostolic order. In only rare instances does his weakness for the "new prophecy" crop out, and then, it is only as one identifies himself with a school within the church. Precisely so Fenelon maintained his milder Montanism, without a thought of deserting the Latin Church. Afterwards Fenelon drew back, but at last poor Tertullian fell away. So with the Jansenists. They credited the *miracles* and the *convulsions* (or ecstasies) of their school, and condemned those who rejected them, as Tertullian condemns the *Psychics*. The great expounder of the Nicene Faith (Bp. Bull) does indeed speak very decidedly of Tertullian as a *lapser*, even when he wrote his first book against Marcion. His semi-schismatic position must be allowed. But, was it a *formal* lapse at that time? The English non-jurors were long in communion with the Church, even while they denounced their brethren and the "Erastianizing" clergy, much as Tertullian does the *Psychics*. St. Augustine speaks of *Tertullianists* with great moderation, and notes the final downfall of our author as something distinct from Tertullianism. When we reflect, therefore, that only four of all his varied writings (now extant) are proofs of an accomplished lapse, ought we not carefully to maintain the distinction between the Montanistic Tertullian and Tertullian the Montanist? Bishop Bull, it seems to me would not object to this way of putting it, when we consider his own discrimination in the following weighty words. He says:

"A clear distinction must be made between those works which Tertullian, when already a Montanist, wrote specifically in defense of Montanism *against the church*, and those which he composed, as a Montanist indeed, yet *not in defense of Montanism against the church*, but rather, *in defense of the common doctrines of the church*—and of Montanus, in opposition to other heretics."

Now in arranging the works of this second class, *the Prescription* comes logically first, because, written in Orthodoxy, it forcibly upholds the Scriptural Rule of Faith, the Catholic touchstone of all professed verity. It is also a necessary Introduction to the great work against Marcion which I have placed next in order; giving it the precedence to which it is entitled in part on chronological ground, in part because of the general purity of its material with the exhibition it presents of the author's mental processes and of his very gradual decline from Truth.

Very fortunate were the Edinburgh Editors in securing for this work and some others, the valuable labors of Dr. Holmes, of whom I have elsewhere given some biographical particulars. The merit and fullness of his annotations are so marked, that I have been spared a great deal of work, such as I was forced to bestow on the former volumes of this American Edition. But on the other hand these pages have given me much patient study and toil as an editor, because of the "shreds and patches" in which Tertullian comes to us, in the Edinburgh Series; and because of some typographical peculiarities, exceptional in that Series itself, and presenting complications, when transferred to a new form of mechanical arrangement.

For example, apart from some valuable material which belongs to the General Preface, and which I have transferred accordingly, the following dislocations confronted me to begin with: The *Marcion* is presented to us in Volume VII. apart from the other writings of Tertullian. At the close of Vol. XI. we reach the *Ad Nationes*, of which Dr. Holmes is the translator, another hand (Mr. Thelwall's) having been employed on former pages of that volume. It is not till we reach Volume XV. that Tertullian again appears, but this volume is wholly the work of Dr. Holmes. Finally, in Volume XVIII., we meet Tertullian again, (Mr. Thelwall the able translator), but, here is placed the "Introduction" to all the works of Tertullian, which, of course, I have, transferred to its proper place. I make these explanations by no means censoriously, but to point out at once the nature of my own task, and the advantage that accrues to the reader, by the order in which the works of the great Tertullian appear in this edition, enabling him to compare different or parallel passages, all methodically arranged in consecutive pages, without a minute's search, or delay.

Now, as to typographical difficulties to which I have referred, Dr. Holmes marks all his multiplied and useful notes with *brackets*, which are almost always superfluous, and which in this American Edition are used to designate my own contributions, when printed with the text, or apart from Preface and Elucidations. These, therefore, I have removed necessarily and with no appreciable loss to the work, but great gain to the

beauty of the page. But, again, Dr. Holmes' translations are all so heavily bracketed as to become an eyesore, and the disfigured pages have been often complained of as afflictive to the reader. Many words strictly implied by the original Latin, and which should therefore be unmarked, are yet put between brackets. Even minute words (*and*, or *to wit*, or *again*,) when, in the nature of the case the English idiom requires them, are thus marked. I have not retained these blemishes; but when an inconsiderable word or a repetition does add to the sense, or qualify it, I have italicized such words, throwing more important interpolations into parenthetical marks, which are less painful to the sight than brackets. I have found them quite as serviceable to denote the auxiliary word or phrase; and where the author himself uses a parenthesis, I have observed very few instances in which a sensible reader would confound it with the translator's efforts to eke out the sense. Sometimes, an awkward interpolation has been thrown into a footnote.
Occasionally the crabbed sentences of the great Carthaginian are so obscure that Dr. Holmes has been unable to make them lucid, although, with the original in hand, he probably felt a force in his own rendering which the mere English reader must fail to perceive. In a few such instances, noting the fact in the margin, I have tried to bring out the sense, by slight modifications of punctuation and arrangement. Occasionally too I have dropped a superfluous interpolation (such as *e.g.*, *to conclude*, or let me say again,) when I have found that it only served to clog and overcharge a sentence. Last of all, Dr. Holmes' *headings* have sometimes been condensed, to avoid phrases and sentences immediately recurring in the chapter. These purely mechanical parts require a terse form of statement, like those in the English Bible, and I have frequently reduced them on that model, dropping redundant adverbs and adjectives to bring out the catchwords.

On Prayer.

Chapter I.—General Introduction.

The Spirit of God, and the Word of God, and the Reason of God—Word of Reason, and Reason and Spirit of Word—Jesus Christ our Lord, namely, who is both the one and the other—has determined for us, the disciples of the New Testament, a new form of prayer; for in this particular also it was needful that new wine should be laid up in new skins, and a new breadth be sewn to a new garment. Besides, whatever had been in bygone days, has either been quite changed, as circumcision; or else supplemented, as the rest of the Law; or else fulfilled, as Prophecy; or else perfected, as faith itself. For the new grace of God has renewed all things from carnal unto spiritual, by super inducing the Gospel, the obliterator of the whole ancient bygone system; in which our Lord Jesus Christ has been approved as the Spirit of God, and the Word of God, and the Reason of God: the Spirit, by which He was mighty; the Word, by which He taught; the Reason, by which He came. So the prayer composed by Christ has been composed of three parts. In speech, by which prayer is enunciated, in spirit, by which alone it prevails, even John had taught his disciples to pray, but all John's doings were laid as groundwork for Christ, until, when "He had increased"—just as the same John used to fore-announce "that it was needful" that "He should increase and himself decrease"—the whole work of the forerunner passed over, together with his spirit itself, unto the Lord. Therefore, after what form of words John taught to pray is not extant, because earthly things have given place to heavenly. "He who is from the earth," says John, "speaketh earthly things; and He who is here from the heavens speaketh those things which He hath seen." And what is the Lord Christ's—as this method of praying is—that is not heavenly? And so, blessed brethren, let us consider His heavenly wisdom: first, touching the precept of praying secretly, whereby He exacted man's faith, that he should be confident that the sight and hearing of Almighty God are present beneath roofs, and extend even into the secret place; and required modesty in faith, that it should offer its religious homage to Him alone, whom it believed to see and to hear everywhere. Further, since wisdom succeeded in the following precept, let it in like manner appertain unto faith, and the modesty of faith, that we think not that the Lord must be approached with a train of words, who, we are certain, takes unsolicited foresight for His own. And yet that very brevity—and let this make for the third grade of wisdom—is supported on the substance of a great and blessed interpretation, and is as diffuse in meaning as it is compressed in words. For it has embraced not only the special duties of prayer, be it veneration of God or petition for man, but almost every discourse of the Lord, every record of His Discipline; so that, in fact, in the Prayer is comprised an epitome of the whole Gospel.

Chapter II—The First Clause.

The prayer begins with a testimony to God, and with the reward of faith, when we say, "Our Father who art in the heavens;" for (in so saying), we at once pray to God, and commend faith, whose reward this appellation is. It is written, "To them who believed on Him He gave power to be called sons of God." However, our Lord very frequently proclaimed God as a Father to us; nay, even gave a precept "that we call no one on earth father, but the Father whom we have in the heavens:" and so, in thus praying, we are likewise obeying the precept. Happy they who recognize their Father! This is the reproach that is brought against Israel, to which the Spirit attests heaven and earth, saying, "I have begotten sons, and they have not recognized me." Moreover, in saying "Father," we also call Him "God." That appellation is one both of filial duty and of power. Again, in the Father the Son is invoked;

"for I," saith He, "and the Father are One." Nor is even our mother the Church passed by, if, that is, in the Father and the Son is recognized the mother, from whom arises the name both of Father and of Son. In one general term, then, or word, we both honor God, together with His own, and are mindful of the precept, and set a mark on such as have forgotten their Father.

Chapter III—The Second Clause.

The name of "God the Father" had been published to none. Even Moses, who had interrogated Him on that very point, had heard a different name. To us it has been revealed in the Son, for the Son is now the Father's new name. "I am come," saith He, "in the Father's name;" and again, "Father, glorify Thy name;" and more openly, "I have manifested Thy name to men." That name, therefore, we pray may "be hallowed." Not that it is becoming for men to wish God well, as if there were any other by whom He may be wished well, or as if He would suffer unless we do so wish. Plainly, it is universally becoming for God to be blessed in every place and time, on account of the memory of His benefits ever due from every man. But this petition also serves the turn of a blessing. Otherwise, when is the name of God not "holy," and "hallowed" through Himself, seeing that of Himself He sanctifies all others—He to whom that surrounding circle of angels cease not to say, "Holy, holy, holy?" In likewise, therefore, we too, candidates for angelhood, if we succeed in deserving it, begin even here on earth to learn by heart that strain hereafter to be raised unto God, and the function of future glory. So far, for the glory of God. On the other hand, for our own petition, when we say, "Hallowed be Thy name," we pray this; that it may be hallowed in us who are in Him, as well in all others for whom the grace of God is still waiting; that we may obey this precept, too, in "praying for all," even for our personal enemies. And therefore with suspended utterance, not saying, "Hallowed be it in us," we say—"in all."

Chapter IV—The Third Clause.

According to this model, we subjoin, "Thy will be done in the heavens and on the earth;" not that there is some power withstanding to prevent God's will being done, and we pray for Him the successful achievement of His will; but we pray for His will to be done in all. For, by figurative interpretation of flesh and spirit, we are "heaven" and "earth;" albeit, even if it is to be understood simply, still the sense of the petition is the same, that in us God's will be done on earth, to make it possible, namely, for it to be done also in the heavens. What, moreover, does God will, but that we should walk according to His Discipline? We make petition, then, that He supply us with the substance of His will, and the capacity to do it, that we may be saved both in the heavens and on earth; because the sum of His will is the salvation of them whom He has adopted. There is, too, that will of God which the Lord accomplished in preaching, in working, in enduring: for if He Himself proclaimed that He did not His own, but the Father's will, without doubt those things which He used to do were the Father's will; unto which things, as unto exemplars, we are now provoked; to preach, to work, to endure even unto death. And we need the will of God, that we may be able to fulfil these duties. Again, in saying, "Thy will be done," we are even wishing well to ourselves, in so far that there is nothing of evil in the will of God; even if, proportionally to each one's deserts, somewhat other is imposed on us. So by this expression we premonish our own selves unto patience. The Lord also, when He had wished to demonstrate to us, even in His own flesh, the flesh's infirmity, by the reality of suffering, said, "Father, remove this Thy cup;" and remembering Himself, added, "save that not my will, but Thine be done." Himself was the Will and the Power of the Father: and yet, for the demonstration of the patience which was due, He gave Himself up to the Father's Will.

Chapter V—The Fourth Clause.

"Thy kingdom come" has also reference to that whereto "Thy will be done" refers—in us, that is. For when does God not reign, in whose hand is the heart of all kings? But whatever we wish for ourselves we augur for Him, and to Him we attribute what from Him we expect. And so, if the manifestation of the Lord's kingdom pertains unto the will of God and unto our anxious expectation, how do some pray for some protraction of the age, when the kingdom of God, which we pray may arrive, tends unto the consummation of the age? Our wish is, that our reign be hastened, not our servitude protracted. Even if it had not been prescribed in the Prayer that we should ask for the advent of the kingdom, we should, unbidden, have sent forth that cry, hastening toward the realization of our hope. The souls of the martyrs beneath the altar cry in jealousy unto the Lord, "How long, Lord, dost Thou not avenge our blood on the inhabitants of the earth?" for, of course, their avenging is regulated by the end of the age. Nay, Lord, Thy kingdom come with all speed—the prayer of Christians the confusion of the heathen, the exultation of angels, for the sake of which we suffer, nay, rather, for the sake of which we pray!

Chapter VI—The Fifth Clause.

But how gracefully has the Divine Wisdom arranged the order of the prayer; so that after things heavenly—that is, after the "Name" of God, the "Will" of God, and the "Kingdom" of God—it should give earthly necessities also room for a petition! For the Lord had withal issued His edict, "Seek ye first the kingdom, and then even these shall be added:" albeit we may rather understand, "Give us this day our daily bread," spiritually. For Christ is our Bread; because Christ is Life, and bread is life. "I am," saith He, "the Bread of

Life;" and, a little above, "The Bread is the Word of the living God, who came down from the heavens." Then we find, too, that His body is reckoned in bread: "This is my body." And so, in petitioning for "daily bread," we ask for perpetuity in Christ, and indivisibility from His body. But, because that word is admissible in a carnal sense too, it cannot be so used without the religious remembrance withal of spiritual Discipline; for (the Lord) commands that bread be prayed for, which is the only food necessary for believers; for "all other things the nations seek after." The like lesson He both inculcates by examples, and repeatedly handles in parables, when He says, "Doth a father take away bread from his children, and hand it to dogs?" and again, "Doth a father give his son a stone when he asks for bread?" For He thus shows what it is that sons expect from their father. Nay, even that nocturnal knocker knocked for "bread." Moreover, He justly added, "Give us this day," seeing He had previously said, "Take no careful thought about the morrow, what ye are to eat." To which subject He also adapted the parable of the man who pondered on an enlargement of his barns for his forthcoming fruits, and on seasons of prolonged security; but that very night he dies.

Chapter VII—The Sixth Clause.

It was suitable that, after contemplating the liberality of God, we should likewise address His clemency. For what will aliments profit us, if we are really consigned to them, as it were a bull destined for a victim? The Lord knew Himself to be the only guiltless One, and so He teaches that we beg "to have our debts remitted us." A petition for pardon is a full confession; because he who begs for pardon fully admits his guilt. Thus, too, penitence is demonstrated acceptable to God who desires it rather than the death of the sinner. Moreover, debt is, in the Scriptures, a figure of guilt; because it is equally due to the sentence of judgment, and is exacted by it: nor does it evade the justice of exaction, unless the exaction be remitted, just as the lord remitted to that slave in the parable his debt; for hither does the scope of the whole parable tend. For the fact withal, that the same servant, after liberated by his lord, does not equally spare his own debtor; and, being on that account impeached before his lord, is made over to the tormentor to pay the uttermost farthing—that is, every guilt, however small: corresponds with our profession that "we also remit to our debtors;" indeed elsewhere, too, in conformity with this Form of Prayer, He saith, "Remit, and it shall be remitted you." And when Peter had put the question whether remission was to be granted to a brother seven times, "Nay," saith He, "seventy-seven times;" in order to remold the Law for the better; because in Genesis vengeance was assigned "seven times" in the case of Cain, but in that of Lamech "seventy-seven times."

Chapter VIII—The Seventh or Final Clause.

For the completeness of so brief a prayer He added—in order that we should supplicate not touching the remitting merely, but touching the entire averting, of acts of guilt—"Lead us not into temptation:" that is, suffer us not to be led into it, by him (of course) who tempts; but far be the thought that the Lord should seem to tempt, as if He either were ignorant of the faith of any, or else were eager to overthrow it. Infirmity and malice are characteristics of the devil. For God had commanded even Abraham to make a sacrifice of his son, for the sake not of tempting, but proving, his faith; in order through him to make an example for that precept of His, whereby He was, by and by, to enjoin that he should hold no pledges of affection dearer than God. He Himself, when tempted by the devil, demonstrated who it is that presides over and is the originator of temptation. This passage He confirms by subsequent ones, saying, "Pray that ye be not tempted;" yet they were tempted, (as they showed) by deserting their Lord, because they had given way rather to sleep than prayer. The final clause, therefore, is consonant, and interprets the sense of

"Lead us not into temptation;" for this sense is, "But convey us away from the Evil One."

Chapter IX—Recapitulation.

In summaries of so few words, how many utterances of the prophets, the Gospels, the apostles—how many discourses, examples, parables of the Lord, are touched on! How many duties are simultaneously discharged! The honor of God in the "Father;" the testimony of faith in the "Name;" the offering of obedience in the "Will;" the commemoration of hope in the "Kingdom;" the petition for life in the "Bread;" the full acknowledgment of debts in the prayer for their "Forgiveness;" the anxious dread of temptation in the request for "Protection." What wonder? God alone could teach how he wished Himself prayed to. The religious rite of prayer therefore, ordained by Himself, and animated, even at the moment when it was issuing out of the Divine mouth, by His own Spirit, ascends, by its own prerogative, into heaven, commending to the Father what the Son has taught.

Chapter X—We May Super add Prayers of Our Own to the Lord's Prayer.

Since, however, the Lord, the Foreseer of human necessities, said separately, after delivering His Rule of Prayer, "Ask, and ye shall receive;" and since there are petitions which are made according to the circumstances of each individual; our additional wants have the right—after beginning with the legitimate and customary prayers as a foundation, as it were—of rearing an outer superstructure of petitions, yet with remembrance of the Master's precepts.

Chapter XI—When Praying the Father, You are Not to Be Angry with a Brother.

That we may not be as far from the ears of God as we are from His precepts, the memory of His precepts paves for our prayers a way unto heaven; of which precepts the chief is, that we go not up unto God's altar before we compose whatever of discord or offence we have contracted with our brethren. For what sort of deed is it to approach the peace of God without peace? the remission of debts while you retain them? How will he appease his Father who is angry with his brother, when from the beginning "all anger" is forbidden us? For even Joseph, when dismissing his brethren for the purpose of fetching their father, said, "And be not angry in the way." He warned us, to be sure, at that time (for elsewhere our Discipline is called "the Way"), that when, set in "the way" of prayer, we go not unto "the Father" with anger. After that, the Lord, "amplifying the Law," openly adds the prohibition of anger against a brother to that of murder. Not even by an evil word does He permit it to be vented. Ever if we must be angry, our anger must not be maintained beyond sunset, as the apostle admonishes. But how rash is it either to pass a day without prayer, while you refuse to make satisfaction to your brother; or else, by perseverance in anger, to lose your prayer?

Chapter XII—We Must Be Free Likewise from All Mental Perturbation.

Nor merely from anger, but altogether from all perturbation of mind, ought the exercise of prayer to be free, uttered from a spirit such as the Spirit unto whom it is sent. For a defiled spirit cannot be acknowledged by a holy Spirit, nor a sad by a joyful, nor a fettered by a free. No one grants reception to his adversary: no one grants admittance except to his compeer.

Chapter XIII—Of Washing the Hands.

But what reason is there in going to prayer with hands indeed washed, but the spirit foul?—inasmuch as to our hands themselves spiritual purities are necessary, that they may be "lifted up pure" from falsehood, from murder, from cruelty, from poisonings, from idolatry, and all the other blemishes which, conceived by the spirit, are effected by the operation of the hands. These are the true purities; not those which most are superstitiously careful about, taking water at every prayer, even when they are coming from a bath of the whole body. When I was scrupulously making a thorough investigation of this practice, and searching into the reason of it, I ascertained it to be a commemorative act, bearing on the surrender of our Lord. We, however, pray to the Lord: we do not surrender Him; nay, we ought even to set ourselves in opposition to the example of His surrenderer, and not, on that account, wash our hands. Unless any defilement contracted in human intercourse be a conscientious cause for washing them, they are otherwise clean enough, which together with our whole body we once washed in Christ.

Chapter XIV—Apostrophe.

Albeit Israel washed daily all his limbs over, yet is he never clean. His hands, at all events, are ever unclean, eternally dyed with the blood of the prophets, and of the Lord Himself; and on that account, as being hereditary culprits from their privity to their fathers' crimes, they do not dare even to raise them unto the Lord, for fear some Isaiah should cry out, for fear Christ should utterly shudder. We, however, not only raise, but even expand them; and, taking our model from the Lord's passion even in prayer we confess to Christ.

Chapter XV—Of Putting Off Cloaks.

But since we have touched on one special point of empty observance, it will not be irksome to set our brand likewise on the other points against which the reproach of vanity may deservedly be laid; if, that is, they are observed without the authority of any precept either of the Lord, or else of the apostles. For matters of this kind belong not to religion, but to superstition, being studied, and forced, and of curious rather than rational ceremony; deserving of restraint, at all events, even on this ground, that they put us on a level with Gentiles. As, e.g., it is the custom of some to make prayer with cloaks doffed, for so do the nations approach their idols; which practice, of course, were its observance becoming, the apostles, who teach concerning the garb of prayer, would have comprehended in their instructions, unless any think that is was in prayer that Paul had left his cloak with Carpus! God, forsooth, would not hear cloaked suppliants, who plainly heard the three saints in the Babylonian king's furnace praying in their trousers and turbans.

Chapter XVI—Of Sitting After Prayer.

Again, for the custom which some have of sitting when prayer is ended, I perceive no reason, except that which children give. For what if that Hermas, whose writing is generally inscribed with the title The Shepherd, had, after finishing his prayer, not sat down on his bed, but done some other thing: should we maintain that also as a matter for observance? Of course not. Why, even as it is the sentence, "When I had prayed, and had sat down on my bed," is simply put with a view to the order of the narration, not as a model of discipline. Else we shall have to pray nowhere except where there is a bed! Nay, whoever sits in a chair or on a bench, will act contrary to that writing. Further: inasmuch as the nations do the like, in sitting down after adoring their petty images;

even on this account the practice deserves to be censured in us, because it is observed in the worship of idols. To this is further added the charge of irreverence—intelligible even to the nations themselves, if they had any sense. If, on the one hand, it is irreverent to sit under the eye, and over against the eye, of him whom you most of all revere and venerate; how much more, on the other hand, is that deed most irreligious under the eye of the living God, while the angel of prayer is still standing by unless we are upbraiding God that prayer has wearied us!

Chapter XVII—Of Elevated Hands.

But we more commend our prayers to God when we pray with modesty and humility, with not even our hands too loftily elevated, but elevated temperately and becomingly; and not even our countenance over-boldly uplifted. For that publican who prayed with humility and dejection not merely in his supplication, but in his countenance too, went his way "more justified" than the shameless Pharisee. The sounds of our voice, likewise, should be subdued; else, if we are to be heard for our noise, how large windpipes should we need! But God is the hearer not of the voice, but of the heart, just as He is its inspector. The demon of the Pythian oracle says:

"And I do understand the mute, and plainly hear the speechless one."

Do the ears of God wait for sound? How, then, could Jonah's prayer find way out unto heaven from the depth of the whale's belly, through the entrails of so huge a beast; from the very abysses, through so huge a mass of sea? What superior advantage will they who pray too loudly gain, except that they annoy their neighbors? Nay, by making their petitions audible, what less error do they commit than if they were to pray in public?

Chapter XVIII—Of the Kiss of Peace.

Another custom has now become prevalent. Such as are fasting withhold the kiss of peace, which is the seal of prayer, after prayer made with brethren. But when is peace more to be concluded with brethren than when, at the time of some religious observance, our prayer ascends with more acceptability; that they may themselves participate in our observance, and thereby be mollified for transacting with their brother touching their own peace? What prayer is complete if divorced from the "holy kiss?" Whom does peace impede when rendering service to his Lord? What kind of sacrifice is that from which men depart without peace? Whatever our prayer be, it will not be better than the observance of the precept by which we are bidden to conceal our fasts; for now, by abstinence from the kiss, we are known to be fasting. But even if there be some reason for this practice, still, lest you offend against this precept, you may perhaps defer your "peace" at home, where it is not possible for your fast to be entirely kept secret. But wherever else you can conceal your observance, you ought to remember the precept: thus you may satisfy the requirements of Discipline abroad and of custom at home. So, too, on the day of the Passover, when the religious observance of a fast is general, and as it were public, we justly forego the kiss, caring nothing to conceal anything which we do in common with all.

Chapter XIX—Of Stations.

Similarly, too, touching the days of Stations, most think that they must not be present at the sacrificial prayers, on the ground that the Station must be dissolved by reception of the Lord's Body. Does, then, the Eucharist cancel a service devoted to God, or bind it more to God? Will not your Station be more solemn if you have withal stood at God's altar? When the Lord's Body has been received and reserved each point is secured, both the participation of the sacrifice and the discharge of duty. If the "Station" has received its name from the example of military life—for we withal are God's military—of course no gladness or sadness chanting to the camp abolishes the "stations" of the soldiers: for gladness will carry out discipline more willingly, sadness more carefully.

Chapter XX—Of Women's Dress.

So far, however, as regards the dress of women, the variety of observance compels us—men of no consideration whatever—to treat, presumptuously indeed, after the most holy apostle, except in so far as it will not be presumptuously if we treat the subject in accordance with the apostle. Touching modesty of dress and ornamentation, indeed, the prescription of Peter likewise is plain, checking as he does with the same mouth, because with the same Spirit, as Paul, the glory of garments, and the pride of gold, and the meretricious elaboration of the hair.

Chapter XXI—Of Virgins.

But that point which is promiscuously observed throughout the churches, whether virgins ought to be veiled or no, must be treated of. For they who allow to virgins immunity from head-covering, appear to rest on this; that the apostle has not defined "virgins" by name, but "women," as "to be veiled;" nor the sex generally, so as to say "females," but a class of the sex, by saying "women:" for if he had named the sex by saying "females," he would have made his limit absolute for everywoman; but while he names one class of the sex, he separates another class by being silent. For, they say, he might either have named "virgins" specially; or generally, by a compendious term, "females."

Chapter XXII—Answer to the Foregoing Arguments.

They who make this concession ought to reflect on the nature of the word itself—what is the meaning of "woman" from the very first records of the sacred writings. Here they find it to be the name of the sex, not a class of the sex: if, that is, God gave to Eve, when she had not yet known a man, the surname "woman" and "female"—("female," whereby the sex generally; "woman," hereby a class of the sex, is marked). So, since at that time the as yet unwedded Eve was called by the word "woman," that word has been made common even to a virgin. Nor is it wonderful that the apostle—guided, of course, by the same Spirit by whom, as all the divine Scripture, so that book Genesis, was drawn up—has used the selfsame word in writing "women," which, by the example of Eve unwedded, is applicable too to a "virgin." In fact, all the other passages are in consonance herewith. For even by this very fact, that he has not named "virgins" (as he does in another place where he is teaching touching marrying), he sufficiently predicates that his remark is made touching everywoman, and touching the whole sex; and that there is no distinction made between a "virgin" and any other, while he does not name her at all. For he who elsewhere—namely, where the difference requires—remembers to make the distinction, (moreover, he makes it by designating each species by their appropriate names,) wishes, where he makes no distinction (while he does not name each), no difference to be understood. What of the fact that in the Greek speech, in which the apostle wrote his letters, it is usual to say, "women" rather than "females;" that is, γυναῖκας (gunaikas) rather than θηλείας (theleias)? Therefore if that word, which by interpretation represents what "female" (femina) represents, is frequently used instead of the name of the sex, he has named the sex in saying γυναῖκα; but in the sex even the virgin is embraced. But, withal, the declaration is plain: "Everywoman," saith he, "praying and prophesying with head uncovered, dishonored her own head." What is "everywoman," but woman of every age, of every rank, of every condition? By saying "every" he excepts naught of womanhood, just as he excepts naught of manhood either from not being covered; for just so he says, "Every man." As, then, in the masculine sex, under the name of "man" even the "youth" is forbidden to be veiled; so, too, in the feminine, under the name of "woman," even the "virgin" is bidden to be veiled. Equally in each sex let the younger age follow the discipline of the elder; or else let the male "virgins," too, be veiled, if the female virgins withal are not veiled, because they are not mentioned by name. Let "man" and "youth" be different, if "woman" and "virgin" are different. For indeed it is "on account of the angels" that he saith women must be veiled, because on account of "the daughters of men" angels revolted from God. Who then, would contend that "women" alone—that is, such as were already wedded and had lost their virginity—were the objects of angelic concupiscence, unless "virgins" are incapable of excelling in beauty and finding lovers? Nay, let us see whether it were not virgins alone whom they lusted after; since Scriptures saith "the daughters of men;" inasmuch as it might have named "wives of men," or "females," indifferently. Likewise, in that it saith, "And they took them to themselves for wives," it does so on this ground, that, of course, such are "received for wives" as are devoid of that title. But it would have expressed itself differently concerning such as were not thus devoid. And so (they who are named) are devoid as much of widowhood as of virginity. So completely has Paul by naming the sex generally, mingled "daughters" and species together in the genus. Again, while he says that "nature herself," which has assigned hair as a tegument and ornament to women, "teaches that veiling is the duty of females," has not the same tegument and the same honor of the head been assigned also to virgins? If "it is shameful" for a woman to be shorn it is similarly so to a virgin too. From them, then, to whom is assigned one and the same law of the head, one and the same discipline of the head is exacted—(which extends) even unto those virgins whom their childhood defends, for from the first a virgin was named "female." This custom, in short, even Israel observes; but if Israel did not observe it, our Law, amplified and supplemented, would vindicate the addition for itself; let it be excused for imposing the veil on virgins also. Under our dispensation, let that age which is ignorant of its sex retain the privilege of simplicity. For both Eve and Adam, when it befell them to be "wise," forthwith veiled what they had learnt to know. At all events, with regard to those in whom girlhood has changed (into maturity), their age ought to remember its duties as to nature, so also, to discipline; for they are being transferred to the rank of "women" both in their persons and in their functions. No one is a "virgin" from the time when she is capable of marriage; seeing that, in her, age has by that time been wedded to its own husband, that is, to time. "But some particular virgin has devoted herself to God. From that very moment she both changes the fashion of her hair, and converts all her garb into that of a 'woman.'" Let her, then, maintain the character wholly, and perform the whole function of a "virgin:" what she conceals for the sake of God, let her cover quite over. It is our business to entrust to the knowledge of God alone that which the grace of God effects in us, lest we receive from man the reward we hope for from God. Why do you denude before God what you cover before men? Will you be more modest in public than in the church? If your self-devotion is a grace of God, and you have received it, "why do you boast," saith he, "as if you have not received it?" Why, by your ostentation of yourself, do you judge others? Is it that, by your boasting, you invite others unto good? Nay, but even you yourself run the risk of losing, if you boast; and you drive others unto the same perils! What is assumed from love of boasting is easily destroyed. Be veiled, virgin, if virgin you are; for you ought to blush. If you are a virgin, shrink from (the gaze of) many eyes. Let no one wonder at your face; let no one perceive your falsehood. You do well in falsely assuming the married character, if you veil your head; nay, you do not seem to assume it falsely, for you are wedded to Christ: to Him you have surrendered your body; act as becomes your Husband's discipline. If He bids the brides of others to be veiled, His own, of course, much more. "But each individual man is not to think that the institution of his predecessor is to be overturned." Many yield up their own judgment, and its consistency, to the custom of others. Granted that virgins be not compelled to be veiled, at all events such as voluntarily are so should not be prohibited; who, likewise, cannot deny themselves to be virgins, content, in the security of a good conscience before God, to damage their own fame. Touching such, however, as are betrothed, I can with constancy "above my small measure" pronounce and attest that they are to be veiled from that day forth on which they shuddered at the first bodily touch of a man by kiss and hand. For in them everything has been fore wedded: their age, through maturity; their flesh, through age; their spirit, through consciousness; their modesty, through the experience of the kiss their hope, through expectation; their mind through volition. And Rebecca is example enough for us, who, when her betrothed had been pointed out, veiled herself for marriage merely on recognition of him.

Chapter XXIII—Of Kneeling.

In the matter of kneeling also prayer is subject to diversity of observance, through the act of some few who abstain from kneeling on the Sabbath; and since this dissension is particularly on its trial before the churches, the Lord will give His grace that the dissentients may either yield, or else indulge their opinion without offence to others. We, however (just as we have received), only on the day of the Lord's Resurrection ought to guard not only against kneeling, but every posture and office of solicitude; deferring even our businesses lest we give any place to the devil. Similarly, too, in the period of Pentecost; which period we distinguish by the same solemnity of exultation. But who would hesitate every day to prostrate himself before God, at least in the first prayer with which we enter on the daylight? At fasts, moreover, and Stations, no prayer should be made without kneeling, and the remaining customary marks of humility; for (then) we are not only praying, but deprecating, and making satisfaction to God our Lord. Touching times of prayer nothing at all has been prescribed, except clearly "to pray at every time and every place."

Chapter XXIV—Of Place for Prayer.

But how "in every place," since we are prohibited (from praying) in public? In every place, he means, which opportunity or even necessity, may have rendered suitable: for that which was done by the apostles (who, in jail, in the audience of the prisoners, "began praying and singing to God") is not considered to have been done contrary to the precept; nor yet that which was done by Paul, who in the ship, in presence of all, "made thanksgiving to God."

Chapter XXV—Of Time for Prayer.

Touching the time, however, the extrinsic observance of certain hours will not be unprofitable—those common hours, I mean, which mark the intervals of the day—the third, the sixth, the ninth—which we may find in the Scriptures to have been more solemn than the rest. The first infusion of the Holy Spirit into the congregated disciples took place at "the third hour." Peter, on the day on which he experienced the vision of Universal Community, (exhibited) in that small vessel, had ascended into the loftier parts of the house, for prayer's sake "at the sixth hour." The same (apostle) was going into the temple, with John, "at the ninth hour," when he restored the paralytic to his health. Albeit these practices stand simply without any precept for their observance, still it may be granted a good thing to establish some definite presumption, which may both add stringency to the admonition to pray, and may, as it were by a law, tear us out from our businesses unto such a duty; so that—what we read to have been observed by Daniel also, in accordance (of course) with Israel's discipline—we pray at least not less than thrice in the day, debtors as we are to Three—Father, Son, and Holy Spirit: of course, in addition to our regular prayers which are due, without any admonition, on the entrance of light and of night. But, withal, it becomes believers not to take food, and not to go to the bath, before interposing a prayer; for the refreshments and nourishments of the spirit are to be held prior to those of the flesh, and things heavenly prior to things earthly.

Chapter XXVI—Of the Parting of Brethren.

You will not dismiss a brother who has entered your house without prayer—"Have you seen," says Scripture, "a brother? you have seen your Lord;"—especially "a stranger," lest perhaps he be "an angel." But again, when received yourself by brethren, you will not make earthly refreshments prior to heavenly, for your faith will forthwith be judged. Or else how will you—according to the precept—say, "Peace to this house," unless you exchange mutual peace with them who are in the house?

Chapter XXVII—Of Subjoining a Psalm.

The more diligent in prayer are wont to subjoin in their prayers the "Hallelujah," and such kind of psalms, in the closes of which the company respond. And, of course, every institution is excellent which, for the extolling and honoring of God, aims unitedly to bring Him enriched prayer as a choice victim.

Chapter XXVIII—Of the Spiritual Victim, Which Prayer is.

For this is the spiritual victim which has abolished the pristine sacrifices. "To what purpose," saith He, "(bring ye) me the multitude of your sacrifices? I am full of holocausts of rams, and I desire not the fat of rams, and the blood of bulls and of goats. For who hath required these from your hands?" What, then, God has required the Gospel teaches. "An hour will come," saith He, "when the true adorers shall adore the Father in spirit and truth. For God is a Spirit, and accordingly requires His adorers to be such." We are the true adorers and the true priests, who, praying in spirit, sacrifice, in spirit, prayer—a victim proper and acceptable to God, which assuredly He has required, which He has looked forward to for Himself! This victim, devoted from the whole heart, fed on faith, tended by truth, entire in innocence, pure in chastity, garlanded with love, we ought to escort with the pomp of good works, amid psalms and hymns, unto God's altar, to obtain for us all things from God.

Chapter XXIX—Of the Power of Prayer.

For what has God, who exacts it ever denied to prayer coming from "spirit and truth?" How mighty specimens of its efficacy do we read, and hear, and believe! Old-world prayer, indeed, used to free from fires, and from beasts, and from famine; and yet it had not (then) received its form from Christ. But how far more amply operative is Christian prayer! It does not station the angel of dew in mid-fires, nor muzzle lions, nor transfer to the hungry the rustics' bread; it has no delegated grace to avert any sense of suffering; but it supplies the suffering, and the feeling, and the grieving, with endurance: it amplifies grace by virtue, that faith may know what she obtains from the Lord, understanding what—for God's name's sake—she suffers. But in days gone by, withal prayer used to call down plagues, scatter the armies of foes, withhold the wholesome influences of the showers. Now, however, the prayer of righteousness averts all God's anger, keeps bivouac on behalf of personal enemies, makes supplication on behalf of persecutors. Is it wonder if it knows how to extort the rains of heaven—(prayer) which was once able to procure its fires? Prayer is alone that which vanquishes God. But Christ has willed that it be operative for no evil: He had conferred on it all its virtue in the cause of good. And so it knows nothing save how to recall the souls of the departed from the very path of death, to transform the weak, to restore the sick, to purge the possessed, to open prison-bars, to loose the bonds of the innocent. Likewise, it washes away faults, repels temptations, extinguishes persecutions, consoles the faint-spirited, cheers the high-spirited, escorts travelers, appeases waves, makes robbers stand aghast, nourishes the poor, governs the rich, upraises the fallen, arrests the falling, confirms the standing. Prayer is the wall of faith: her arms and missiles against the foe who keeps watch over us on all sides. And, so never walk we unarmed. By day, be we mindful of Station; by night, of vigil. Under the arms of prayer guard we the standard of our General; await we in prayer the angel's trump. The angels, likewise, all pray; every creature prays; cattle and wild beasts pray and bend their knees; and when they issue from their layers and lairs, they look up heavenward with no idle mouth, making their breath vibrate after their own manner. Nay, the birds too, rising out of the nest, upraise themselves heavenward, and, instead of hands, expand the cross of their wings, and say somewhat to seem like prayer. What more then, touching the office of prayer? Even the Lord Himself prayed; to whom be honor and virtue unto the ages of the ages!

www.ingramcontent.com/pod-product-compliance
Lightning Source LLC
Chambersburg PA
CBHW071015120726
47910CB00004B/1530

* 9 7 8 1 6 4 3 7 3 0 8 8 2 *